LUDWIG MIES VAN DER ROHE

THE MASTERS OF
WORLD ARCHITECTURE SERIES
UNDER THE GENERAL EDITORSHIP OF WILLIAM ALEX

LE CORBUSIER by Françoise Choay
FRANK LLOYD WRIGHT by Vincent Scully, Jr.
PIER LUIGI NERVI by Ada Louise Huxtable
ANTONIO GAUDÍ by George R. Collins
LUDWIG MIES VAN DER ROHE by Arthur Drexler
ALVAR AALTO by Frederick Gutheim

ludwig mies van der rohe

by Arthur Drexler

George Braziller, Inc.
NEW YORK, 1960

CONTENTS

LUDWIG MIES VAN DER ROHE

THE UTILITARIAN BIAS of the age exalts mediocrity, but it has also found room for three architects of genius: Frank Lloyd Wright, Le Corbusier, and Ludwig Mies van der Rohe.

Wright saw the machine as a tool with which to make buildings approximate natural phenomena: skyscrapers like trees, houses like caves, a museum like a shell. For Le Corbusier technology and art alike derive from geometric form, valuable for its own sake; for him there is no conflict between art and technology, and the machine is no less refreshing than nature. But Mies has responded differently. He has made art seem rational, as if it were science.

The key to Mies' enormous authority lies in one simple fact: his ideas can be taught. His art is communicable. It can be practiced by others with measurable success. The Miesian discipline has attracted architects of every degree of talent, and Mies does not disdain an academy. For Mies architecture is merely the visible expression of a point of view which others naturally will want to share.

It may also be said of Mies that he is the architect *par excellence* of civilization, of law and order, of the great metropolis; in the poetic Spenglerian sense he is the architect of the Universal State, striving to preserve and renew old values. His architecture seeks an absolute and unvarying principle, assumed to be independent of the senses through which its manifestations are perceived. Plato would not be ill at ease in the Miesian world of form.

Mies himself has presented his work on philosophical grounds, discouraging straightforward consideration of its aesthetic character. But Mies is not a philosopher or a theologian; he is first of all an artist. This does not mean that his aesthetic predilections necessarily determine his philosophy. For Mies the aesthetic experience seems rather to serve as an intermediate term within the sequence of an argument. Mies builds as if logic, universal truth, and technology were all *real* things. He makes us believe in them, as he sees them, by the intermediary of art— of sense perceptions placed in the service of ideas. Mies builds as if technology means only post and lintel construction; as if logic means only the multiplication and refinement of distinctions; as if truth means only that general term which can account for the greatest number of particular cases. His buildings achieve greatness when the "as if" is so convincing that we believe in the reality of abstractions; when the visible world no longer suggests a discrepancy between what ought to be and what is. With the subtlety of a theologian Mies makes buildings like aphorisms, each one revealing something we recognize as truth. If buildings may be judged as embodiments of a viable system of ideas, the buildings of Mies van der Rohe are among the most successful in history.

IRON AND GLASS had appeared as significant architectural materials in the middle of the nineteenth century, but by 1910 architecture still meant styles derived from the past. Within these styles the new materials were hidden or distorted. Architecture remained an exercise separate from the facts of structure, and the most significant buildings were railroad stations, bridges, and exhibition halls designed by engineers.

The English Arts and Crafts movement attempted a re-integration, in life as in art, through a return to medieval styles and a substitute for the guild system. But by rejecting the machine the movement lost contact with the society it hoped to influence. In the 1890s *Art Nouveau* made the first attempt to break with all past styles. For a brief time it imposed on architecture and the applied arts curvilinear motifs derived from plant forms and Japanese prints. In architecture the decorative curves of this style were not sustained by any necessity of structure; *Art Nouveau's* success was short-lived.

But the movement led to a new cooperation between art and industry. Peter Behrens and Richard Riemerschmid, among its most gifted exponents, were the first industrial designers as the term is now understood. By 1906 Behrens was producing for the AEG, the German electrical industry, factories and offices in which for the first time since the middle ages the structure of a building began to determine its appearance. For much of his inspiration Behrens turned to the simplified Neo-classic forms of Karl Friedrich Schinkel, the brilliant nineteenth-century eclectic whose sense of site and atmosphere transfigured whatever motifs he employed. The pioneering work of Frank Lloyd Wright was not yet well known. In France Auguste Perret had begun his clarification of structural form within classical canons. In Germany the most interesting work was being done by Behrens. To his office came Walter Gropius and Le Corbusier; Mies van der Rohe arrived in 1908.

Figure 1. Riehl House, Neu Babelsberg, Germany, 1907. Dining room.

Ludwig Mies (van der Rohe is his mother's surname) was born in Aachen in 1886. He attended the Cathedral School until he was thirteen and spent two years more at a trade school; at fifteen his formal education ended. His ideas of order and value derive from the medieval scholastics and St. Thomas Aquinas. Craft and the limitations of materials he learned as an apprentice in his father's stone-cutting yard. The ancient buildings he admired most seemed to him beyond style and time, and of a goodness beyond art.

From his fifteenth to his nineteenth year Mies was a draftsman-designer of stucco ornament, for local architects working in the classical modes. In 1905 he went to Berlin; seeking to improve his knowledge of wood he spent two years in the office of Bruno Paul, a skillful decorator and furniture designer. In 1907, when he was twenty-one, he left Paul's office to execute his first commission, designed with a sure hand in a popular "classical" style. A detail of the Riehl house dining room recalls the interest in Japanese architecture shared by Paul, Mies, and others in Europe, and by Wright in America. The wall is panelled to door height

Figure 2. Kroller House, The Hague, Holland, 1912. Project. Drawing.

Figure 3. Kroller House. Project. Model.

Figure 4. Kroller House. Project. Full scale wood and canvas model erected on the actual site.

12

Figure 5. Bismarck Monument, Bingen on the Rhine, Germany, 1912. Project.

and above that treated as a plaster band, as in the temples and teahouses Japanese visitors to Germany had begun to make known. Related attitudes toward design generate comparable details.

Mies' temperament favors precision and thoroughness. Even without the example of Peter Behrens he would have acquired the habit of designing all the hardware to go into his buildings; but Behrens, a designer of industrial products before there were advertising agencies, must have quickened Mies' appreciation of principled design and fine detail. Important to his practical knowledge was the assignment to supervise the construction of Behrens' German Embassy in St. Petersburg. Still more important was the influence of Schinkel, transmitted particularly through Behrens' domestic architecture. The Perls house, built by Mies in 1911, is a dignified homage to Schinkel that might have been rendered by Behrens himself.

Mies had assisted in the design of a house for Mme. H. E. L. J. Kröller, the owner of a famous collection of modern painting. On leaving Behrens' office in 1912 he was invited by Mme. Kröller to live for a year at The Hague while designing his own version of this project. Though never built it was well studied: Mies constructed a full-scale mock-up in canvas and wood. More than any other early work, including his 1912 competition project for a monument to Bismarck, the Kröller house deepens Mies' affinity with Schinkel. The complicated asymmetry of its massing, the continuous articulation of joints to relate separate sections, the repetition at different scales of a dominant set of proportions: all contribute to an atmosphere of romantic serenity. These are effects of form. They do not distort or neglect structure. In some respects they elaborate it; an example is the doubling of piers in the colonnade. But they remain effects added to structure; they are not structure itself.

During his stay in The Hague Mies observed the buildings of Hendrik Petrus Berlage, whose sympathies lay with the cause of structural honesty advocated by Ruskin. Berlage was not particularly concerned with style, or form. He desired merely that supporting and supported elements be self-evident. The medieval ambiance of his work remains difficult to appreciate, but in Mies his dedication to a principle found a ready audience.

After he returned to Berlin in 1913 Mies executed, at the client's request, another house in an eighteenth-century style. He had opened his own office shortly before World War I began. On his return from the war in 1919 he projected one more house in the Schinkel manner, and then, in the same year, embarked on the first of the five projects which established his fame.

Project: office building, Friedrichstrasse, Berlin. 1919. Glass had often served as a precious ornament set within the stone substance of a building. With the development of structural iron and cheap glass it became possible to build an exhibition hall such as the Crystal Palace; but glass had not been considered as the prime material of *serious* architecture. In this project Mies proposed to make architecture of glass alone. The difficulties of a triangular site are exploited by transparent prow-like corners. Although the building is only twenty stories high, vertical recessions divide the facades into narrow and seemingly taller units. The plan alone reveals the logic of these divisions: the building is conceived as three separate towers, linked to a central unit containing elevators and lobbies.

In 1921 Mies completed a second design for a *Glass Skyscraper,* intended this time for an irregular but imaginary site. The plan recalls the free-form relief sculptures of Jean (Hans) Arp. Its curves produce a facade intended to reflect itself. Flat wide sheets of glass facet the curves; where two curves intersect to form a thin prow, reflections are complimented by transparency. Both projects for glass towers demonstrate with the utmost clarity and thoroughness the possibility of an architecture in which shadows are no longer of prime importance. Mies has explained that he arrived at the form of the second building by studying the play of reflections on a model hung outside the window of his office.

Perhaps because of their novel use of glass, other aspects of these projects have been overlooked. In both of them the technique of skeleton construction is implicit, but a structural system is not indicated for either building. Both designs separate and classify different services, but although they are described as "office buildings" their interior space, in the second project even more than the first, is improbable for any purpose. Glass, not a structural system, has determined the character of the space enclosed, and has even influenced the choice of a site.

Project: concrete office building. 1922. Floors projecting beyond the columns are turned up at the edges to form continuous parapets. Windows run like ribbons completely around the structure. There is little interplay of forms: the impact of the design depends on the repetition of stacked concrete trays, interrupted at ground level to make an entrance, and crowned by a thin roof plate. The ribbon window has become a commonplace in modern architecture; it has never been as carefully or convincingly employed as it is in this study. A single refinement rescues it from that inanity which marks its subsequent use: the concrete parapets are shown in Mies' drawing as being thick enough to contain equipment. This arrangement allows the windows to be recessed, produces a play of shadows, and contrasts the solidity of concrete against the weightlessness of glass.

Project: brick country house. 1923. Weight and density, a sense of the substance of which things are made, have always been important to Mies, yet his most famous project explored not substance but space. Frank Lloyd Wright had preceded Mies in extending walls beyond the roof line and introducing glass at the corners of rooms. But Mies' inspiration in this project is not primarily Wrightian. The brick country house reflects the ideas of Theo van Doesburg, the founder and most effective propogandist of the Dutch group of painters, architects, and sculptors called *de Stijl*. In 1922 van Doesburg had lectured in Berlin and at Gropius' Bauhaus in Weimar. His 1918 painting, called *Rhythms of a Russian Dance*, organized vertical and horizontal lines in a staccato rhythm forcing the observer's eye toward the edges of the canvas. The plan of Mies' brick country house bears a startling resemblance to this painting. Axial walls extend indefinitely into the landscape; three disappear outside the limits of the drawing. The roof is an independent plane beneath which walls seem merely to be passing on their way to the horizon. Interior space becomes a fluid medium channeled between planes entirely independent of each other. An immediate consequence is the near destruction of the building as an entity. Interior and exterior space, no longer rigidly opposed, are now simply degrees or modulations of the same thing. Mies has in fact made the individual wall rather than the room itself the unit of architectural composition: a departure without precedent.

Project: concrete country house. 1924. The fifth and last of these famous projects returns to the study of mass. A pinwheel plan segregates the different elements of

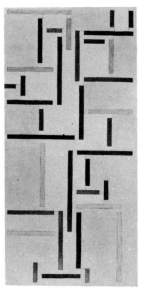

Figure 6. Georges Vantongerloo,
Construction of Volume Relations,
1921. Mahogany. Collection, Museum of Modern Art, New York.

Figure 8. Gerrit Rietveld, Armchair, 1917. Wood
painted red, yellow, blue and black.

a house within distinct zones. Anticipated by Wright, the zoned plan has since been developed, with particular success in the United States, by Marcel Breuer and others. Mies' design is a restless exercise in the centrifugal massing of solids: groups of rooms rather than single walls reach out into the landscape. Extensive cantilevers, and windows cut into both outside and reverse corners, explore the structural possibilities of concrete; they also make ambiguous the distinction between mass and volume. The walls seem to be folded sheets of paper in which rectangular slots have been cut. In this project alone Mies' treatment of the wall, as a surface decorated by holes, is related directly to geometric abstract painting and sculpture.

Like music, architecture must wait for realization on someone other than its author. But there is a paper architecture, a literature of the plan. It includes some of the most important buildings ever designed: in variety of ideas few exceed these five projects. Part of their compelling strength depends on the quality of the drawings themselves. An exquisite rendering of texture and light; a choice of perspectives exaggeratedly calm or attenuated; a sur-real juxtaposition by montage of photographs with flat charcoal or crayon surfaces: these transform ideas into hallucinatory images, beautiful and urgent.

MIES' INNOVATIONS were not isolated phenomena. The years immediately after World War I saw an intellectual quickening in the arts. New movements had begun: *de Stijl* in Holland; Suprematism and Constructivism in Russia; Dadaism in Switzerland; Cubism in France. Of these *de Stijl* was the most directly concerned with an attitude toward form applicable to all the arts.

Moral and philosophical justifications were adduced by van Doesburg and Mondrian for restricting color to flat shades of the primaries. Separate and usually rectangular masses were composed asymmetrically, unified by "occult" balance rather than axial symmetry. In architecture and design a characteristic *Stijl* device was the joining of vertical and horizontal elements so that they seemed to bypass each other. An example is Gerrit Rietveld's famous chair, which he intended as a variation on furniture by Frank Lloyd Wright. These technical devices were applicable to problems of structure, but their real justification was formal: they seemed beautiful and coherent. At the Bauhaus, ideas drawn from *de Stijl* and other movements were given a social significance compatible with the revolutionary spirit of the day, and modified by practical experience.

Architecture had come under the influence of painting and painters. Cubism in France had contributed to Le Corbusier's conception of the house as a *"prisme pur"* raised above the ground. Himself a painter, Le Corbusier used different colors on adjacent walls to demolish or enhance continuity. In this he was anticipated by *de Stijl,* although never with his subtlety or intelligence. Mies, however, preoccupied with more exclusively architectural themes, remained indifferent to the possibilities of applied color.

Mies executed, in 1926, a monument to Karl Liebknecht and Rosa Luxemburg, the founders of the German Communist Party who were killed in a street demonstration in 1919. The monument, demolished by the Nazis, was a wall of Dutch brick. Mies had wanted to make it perfectly flat, but this was thought to be too reticent. He then developed the wall into a large *Stijl* sculpture, piling up heavy rectangular masses in a composition nearly but not quite symmetrical. Stacked like coffins, these dark blocks are all the more oppressive for being arranged with such painstaking irregularity. As an abstract expression of disquiet the monument is unsurpassed—a surprising fact in an age that has afforded so many opportunities.

In 1926 Mies was appointed First Vice-President of the *Deutscher Werkbund,* an organization founded by industrialists and architects to improve the quality of Germany's industrial design. At the *Werkbund's* first exposition, at Cologne in 1914, Gropius built his famous machine hall. For their second exposition in 1927 the *Werkbund* planned to build in Stuttgart a group of houses by the most progressive architects of the day. The project was placed under the direction of Mies. His first version, done shortly before the Liebknecht-Luxemburg monument, grouped houses like blocks and steps on terraces following the contours of the site. There were to be pedestrian streets closed to traffic, and numerous open or partially walled squares.

Despite the personal tastes architects would have brought to the design of individual buildings, Mies' composition probably would have remained intact. However, brick houses executed by Mies in 1926 and 1928 suggest the architectural character he had in mind. The Wolf house is set onto a hillside by means of a podium which is itself part of the wall plane. A garden sunk into the terrace, and a stepped parapet, indicate the variety of sculptural effects Mies was developing. The Esters and Lange houses are of similar interest, particularly in their broad, cubic massing.

Unfortunately the city of Stuttgart wished to sell the houses separately after the exposition closed. Mies produced a more conventional plan for free-standing buildings. As director he brought together some of Europe's most gifted architects, including Behrens, Gropius, J. J. P. Oud, and Le Corbusier. Mies himself designed a small apartment house. Smooth stucco facades and uniform fenestration concealed the variety of its apartment layouts. Its most interesting feature was the vigorous, slightly discordant cantilevering of roofs for the penthouse service units.

MIES SUDDENLY equalled the brilliance of his early theoretical projects with an executed building. As a result of his efforts for the *Deutscher Werkbund* he was commissioned to design the German Pavilion for the International Exposition at Barcelona in 1929. Destroyed when the exposition closed, the building can have been seen by only a few architects or historians concerned with the new style. Subsequent publication established its fame. At the age of forty-three Mies had produced the masterpiece of his European career.

The Barcelona Pavilion, as it has since been called, was without practical purpose. No functional program determined or even influenced its appearance. No part of its interior was taken up by exhibits: the building itself was the object on view. The "exhibition" was an architectural space such as had never been seen. The building consisted of walls and columns arranged on a low travertine podium. Like the 1923 project for a brick country house, it channeled space between separate vertical and horizontal planes. But this time the flow of space was held within clamp-like walls at each end of the podium. Between these walls the building "happened" like a slow dance on a stage.

Apart from the intrinsic beauty of its travertine, gray glass and green marble, the Pavilion's only adornments were furniture specially designed for it by Mies, two reflecting pools lined with black glass, and a sculpture by Georg Kolbe. One other detail was given decorative value: steel columns carrying the roof were sheathed in chrome.

Columns were notably absent from the project for a brick house. In 1922 Mies had seemed indifferent to a major aspect of the new architecture. Steel or concrete columns regularly spaced allowed a new freedom in the disposition of walls, if indeed "walls" were any longer necessary. Le Corbusier's famous diagram of 1914 illustrated what had become the irreducible framework: floor slabs and a flat roof carried by slender columns. Within such a framework walls could be arranged like furniture; on it they could be hung like curtains. But Mies had gone directly to this freedom of composition without the aid of a separate skeleton structure. Its appearance in the Barcelona Pavilion announced a problem.

The Pavilion's walls were placed only a few feet from columns they might just as well have absorbed. The columns were superfluous, and were eliminated from the caretaker's shelter at one end of the podium. But as fixed, regularly spaced elements they introduced an objective order. Against them the eye could measure a space entirely subjective in its organization. The Barcelona Pavilion can fairly be described as one of the first modern buildings able to withstand comparison with the best work of the past. Such a comparison would be to Mies' advantage. Like Le Corbusier's Villa Savoye or Wright's Robie house, the Barcelona Pavilion is more than a unique masterpiece. It is the grammar of a complete style, an ordering principle capable of generating other works of art. But within its discipline is the beginning of that conflict between subjective space and a wholly rational order that has since come to mark Mies' work.

THE APPARENT simplicity of Mies' buildings gives to each object inside them an unprecedented importance. The walls seem to withdraw, leaving chairs and tables on exhibition. Mies has in fact developed the techniques of exhibition installation into a minor art. Characteristically, he builds as much of the installation as possible from the material to be shown; everything else is eliminated. In the 1929 glass exhibit at Stuttgart curved sheets of glass were lined up in squads. The material was merely on view, but in prodigal quantity. Where fixtures are unavoidable Mies expends on them endless attention. Vitrines for the display of printed material in the Berlin Building Exposition are reminiscent of Rietveld's furniture, and

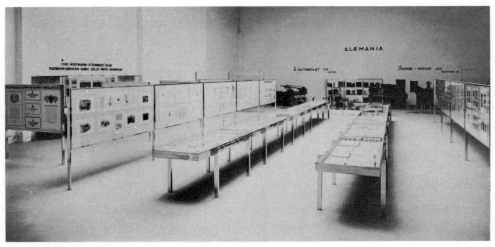

Figure 9. Berlin Building Exposition, 1931.

anticipate a major structural theme: the cabinet and its supports may be recognized as a miniature of the 1950 Farnsworth House.

Mies designed his first chair for the 1927 silk exhibit. Made of bent steel tubes, its cantilevered seat adjusts slightly to the occupant's weight. The armchair version of this design bears a family resemblance to the bent-wood furniture produced from the 1860s onward by Thonet, which company also manufactured Mies' designs. For the Barcelona Pavilion he produced what has been acclaimed the most beautiful of modern chairs. Made of steel bands in single and reverse curves, it requires painstaking craftsmanship to give the illusion of impersonal machine technique. The Barcelona chair is wide and comfortable: its imposing dignity has made it one of modern architecture's few pieces of "monumental" furniture. In the United States today no newly remodelled institution seems able to do without it, and yet despite such familiarity it is unfailingly agreeable to see.

A YOUNG WOMAN whose father had offered to give her a house as a wedding gift was much impressed with one of Mies' early Neo-classic villas. Architects and students must admire Mies' powers of persuasion: the commission resulted in the Tugendhat house in Brno, Czechoslovakia. In 1930 it was one of the most uncompromising statements of the new architecture.

Situated on a sloping site, with a superb view of the town, this building is entered from its top floor. A glass-enclosed stair leads to the living rooms below, where some 100 feet of glass open the house to the view. Alternate panels automatically lower into the basement, converting the living room into a great semi-enclosed terrace. As in the Barecelona Pavilion, subdivisions of space within a single large area are effected chiefly by free-standing walls adjacent to chrome-plated columns. The main seating area of the living room is defined by a single wall of onyx; a large semi-circle of macassar ebony demarcates the dining area. Curtains of black and beige raw silk and white velvet, and furniture exactly placed, also serve as architectural elements. Mies designed all the furniture and every detail, including door handles and curtain tracks. Bedrooms on the upper floor are almost completely conventional in planning, Mies having held to closed, box-like rooms wherever privacy was required. The building is in fact two separate concepts superimposed: the lower level affords an almost ritualistic elegance; the upper level is distinguished chiefly by its convenience.

A more thoroughgoing application of the open plan occurs in a house Mies designed for the Berlin Building Exposition of 1931, which he also directed. Here only the kitchen and servant's quarters are isolated from a continuously flowing space. Two master bedrooms, screened from the living area, are separated from each other only by a partly circular shaft enclosing a bathroom. Regularly placed metal columns are contrasted with freely placed walls, some of them extending well beyond the roof line. The most beautiful use of this device is the walled patio, in which the master suite becomes a lightly sheltered alcove. This was to be the last house by Mies in which individual walls, extending out into the landscape, break up each elevation and tie the building to its site.

MIES PRODUCED from 1931 to 1938 a series of projects for ideal houses in which unbroken exterior walls enclosed house and garden alike. The court house is one of Mies' most elaborately studied themes; in four different designs he has suggested an astonishing variety of effects, and studies made during this period for actual clients develop the theme in specific detail.

The 1931 row house project consists simply of a square court with glass walls arranged to form an L along two sides. Rooms are indicated by cabinet walls and free-standing partitions. The same L plan is repeated for each house, so that no two courts are adjacent. The arrangement suggests a degree of luxury one would not have thought possible for a one story row house.

A 1934 project makes use of not one but three courts. The house proper is again a roofed section of the total walled area. Its plan forms a T, so that each wing looks out on two courts. Interior subdivisions are effected by by-passing walls, but this time there is a greater richness in the modulation of space through numerous turns and alcoves. The Hubbe house project of 1935 carries out a similar conception to the last practical detail.

The 1934 project for a court house with a garage presents a startling innovation. Again, a large rectangular enclosure is made by a masonry wall. The entire area is paved. The house is a pavilion backed up against one wall, with a large court on either side. Mies had previously used curved screen walls to partition rectangular spaces: but in this design two sweeping segments of circles are used to disrupt a rectangular composition. They seem to bend the space in order to accommodate a garage forced into the building along a diagonal axis. The garage is of course a pretext: Mies has used a pseudo-functional problem to justify a space more subjectively determined than any he had yet proposed. The rectangle of the plan becomes a painter's canvas. On it Mies juxtaposes positive and negative intervals, counter-movements and distortions, admitting to architecture a kind and quality of space not normally considered appropriate to it. It is difficult to imagine how space could be used in a more painterly way, or how it could be made to contrast more expressively with a rational, measured structure.

As the court house with a garage might almost have derived from the painting of Kandinsky, the 1938 project for a group of three court houses suggests a characteristic work of Mondrian's. A large rectangle has been divided into three compartments. Within these, two of the court houses appear simply as glass pavilions. The third house, however, itself replaces a wall, and separates adjacent rectangles of different sizes. Interior walls are freely placed in the style of Mies' (and Mondrian's) earlier work. The supporting function of columns is never assigned to interior walls, or integrated with the structural frame of the exterior glass walls. Like a Chinese palace the scheme reveals fascinating pockets and alcoves, courts within courts. Like Chinese architecture too it juxtaposes the satisfactions of the imperturbable wall with the mystery of space, while preserving the order of visible structure.

The court house projects are abstract, suggesting a building type and a procedure. In all of them aesthetic character depends on movement contained within rigid limits. The few simple elements to which Mies has reduced buildings have been admired for their serenity. But the inner movement they provoke is restless and inexorable. The interiors of Mies' most original buildings are like landscapes or city streets. Between their walls the spectator may pause but seldom rest: always there is something around the corner. In the few projects Mies designed before 1938 for groups of buildings, however, the movement of space between individual units is not their most interesting feature. Sculptural mass and density are elaborated in the first project for the *Deutscher Werkbund's* Stuttgart exposition. A static, uneasily defined space is proposed in the 1928 competition project for the remodeling of Berlin's Alexander-platz. In that project also, individual buildings are regularly structured blocks, the horizontal lines of floor slabs and parapets dominating the verticals of columns. A 1933 project for the Reichsbank, and a 1937 project for a silk industry administration building, similarly employ horizontal emphasis with regular skeleton steel structure, but now each building is broken up into flat or curved wings symmetrically grouped. Dry and competent, these designs seem not to have been done by the architect of the Barcelona Pavilion or the court house projects. But with them Mies was quietly preparing a new foundation for his work.

In 1930 Mies was appointed Director of the Bauhaus School at Dessau, and in 1931 he was made a member of the Prussian Academy of Arts and Sciences. A Nazi group in Dessau made it desirable to move the school to Berlin, but in 1933

Mies decided to close it. He left Germany in 1937 and settled in the United States. Shortly thereafter he was appointed Director of Architecture for Armour Institute, now called Illinois Institute of Technology. He became an American citizen in 1944.

It is often said that Mies could have realized his ideas only in the United States, and that only Europe could have produced him. But Mies has seemed more American than the Americans: the Puritan tradition and the transcendental philosophers of nineteenth-century New England must seem sentimental beside Mies himself, and in this sense too his present and most intensely traditional expression of Western values satisfies an American aspiration. His buildings have also corresponded to an American pragmatism. The techniques of steel construction Mies favors have been extensively developed in the United States, and his architecture is pre-eminently buildable. As a result, his influence here has been furthered by the example of actual buildings rather than by unexecuted projects, such as established his first fame. And his American work has attracted followers all over the world (as his European work did not).

The history of Mies' architecture in the United States has involved the gradual exclusion of everything that has seemed to him subjective and conditional. Structure alone is retained, and to structure is assigned a value independent of such particulars as site, function, and to some extent climate and materials. Space and light, so far from being elaborated, are suppressed as decisive architectural experiences. And yet it is not possible to make architecture out of structure alone; it is possible not to eliminate what is subjective but only to rationalize it. Mies' rationalization is among the most convincing ever made. His American work is a contest in which an imaginary absolute triumphs over reality.

THE CONTEST begins with an effort to produce a unified whole from disparate elements, by letting each one develop according to its own nature. The 1942 project for a Museum for a small city derives from the Barcelona Pavilion, but here all exterior walls are of glass and the column structure dominates the entire conception. Interior walls are disposed in counterpoint to the sequence of columns. The composition is as beautiful as it is ill-suited for the requirements of an ordinary museum, since the walls themselves, being kept free of the ceiling in order to emphasize the structural function of the columns, must inevitably be the most interesting objects on view. That Mies intended this is evidenced by a series of montage-drawings showing each wall as a single gigantic picture, rather than as a background for paintings of normal size. The extraordinarily subtle grouping of these walls, together with an auditorium and two roof openings for courtyards, produces a kind of enclosed lanscape. But the unbroken planes of the glass facades insist on a distinction between interior and exterior space, avoided in the Barcelona Pavilion even with its opaque marble walls. Glass here takes on the usual aspect of a facade. Interior walls are free of the roof as well as of the columns; and the columns by sheer number provide a unifying rhythm and pattern. Each element has been allowed to develop fully, and yet the result is a superimposition of separate concepts, no one of them indispensable to the others.

This development is carried further in the 1942 project for a Concert Hall. Here interior columns have been eliminated. They are replaced by a vast steel truss of the sort used in airplane hangars or factories. In the entirely free space this roof makes possible, Mies suspends completely separate wall and ceiling planes. Their arrangement suggests an architecture in which the roof rather than columns provides a fixed modular rhythm, while the wall planes may be so entirely liberated as to float in space and, perhaps, be re-arranged according to the occasion. From the triumvirate of roof plane, columns, and walls Mies has here removed the central element and transformed the other two. Unity now depends on highly developed elements that yet remain only details, and therefore dependent on each other.

This first phase in the contest between the absolute and the conditional takes place on paper. The second phase takes place almost entirely in the realm of practical building. In his designs for the campus of Illinois Institute of Technology Mies produced an overall plan and a series of individual buildings astonishing for both their unity and variety. The entire site is divided into 24-foot modules in both directions. Individual buildings are rectangles proportioned by this module. The initial plan called for the closing of one street: abandoned for various legal reasons, the scheme was replaced by a more conventional one. In the executed as well as the projected versions the space between buildings appears secondary to the buildings themselves. Even the characteristically *de Stijl* by-passing of rectangles in a kind of sliding composition produces only a residual space, however large it may be. The site planning is interesting for its simultaneous development of symmetry and asymmetry; of clusters of identical buildings disposed asymmetrically around formal axes.

Although the buildings individually are aggregates of the 24-foot module, the emphatic treatment of corners tends to obscure their underlying structural regularity. The corner detail is the best known and certainly one of the most influential of Mies' American contributions. The manner in which Mies brings together steel, brick, and glass is made to carry the full burden of the art of architecture. Modulations of interior space, varying intensities of light, and interesting profiles against the sky have all been suppressed or eliminated. In their place the eye "reads" consistent structural detail. A typical corner intersection of brick walls with a steel column requires extra steel angles to articulate the wall as a nonstructural panel. Other steel elements produce a linear division of surface akin to much classical Japanese architecture as well as to the later compositions of Mondrian. But the intense development of the corners of volumes, with their thickening of black steel, provides a termination to these paneled facades closer in spirit to Greek inter-columniation than to the extendable patterns of modern abstract painting. The multiplication of steel elements, often for purposes of dubious structural value, suggests also an affinity with Gothic systems of decoration. Not all of the essential structure is visible; much visible structure is in fact decoration; and the choice of structural system depends on the assumption that it has some intrinsic beauty worth elaborating. There are simpler ways to build with brick and steel, but Mies' system of forms appears at once simple and beautiful.

Of the several buildings Mies has designed for the Illinois Institute of Technology one of the most important remains unbuilt. This is the project for a monu-mental library-administration building with an enormous interior court, a two-story library, and a cantilevered mezzanine within a two-story public space, all organized to present vistas of heroic scale. The glass panels for the exterior walls would have been the largest ever produced in the United States.

Only in this work did Mies explore spacial development within his system of structural articulation. Had it been built the library and administration hall would have ranked as Mies' most brilliant achievement within this series; and had it been built the nature of his influence on American architects might have been considerably different.

What Mies intricately pieces together with many steel elements, other architects reduce to one element more economical to build but less effective visually. Perhaps the one Miesian device that has most often been rendered meaningless by other architects is the famous mullion detail used on the apartment towers at 860 Lake Shore Drive, in Chicago, built in 1951. These towers are glass and steel cages of absolute uniformity, placed at right angles to each other and at oblique angles to the main thoroughfare. Steel mullions to hold the glass are welded to the edge of each floor slab. For consistency mullions are applied to the columns, where they serve no structural purpose. Apart from its classical proportions of three bays to five, and the superb handling of entrances, the buildings' chief refinement is the effect of changing density produced by the mullions. Depending on the angle at which they are seen they may entirely conceal the glass, or, on the contrary, they may become nearly invisible.

These twin towers were preceded by the Promontory apartment house, built in 1949. For this building Mies prepared a version in steel in which applied mullions

Figure 10. Apartment House, 860 Lake Shore Drive, 1951. Photographed in construction; mullions and spandrels being placed in position.

appear for the first time. Unlike later designs, however, the Promontory apartment house is not a pure glass-walled rectangle. It is a thin slab with two wings projecting from it at the rear. The steel version of the Promontory proved too expensive and it was instead executed in concrete. Perimeter columns were placed outside the wall plane and graduated in depth at two story intervals, like buttresses. Their step rhythm lends interest to a facade otherwise distinguished only for its orderliness.

The massing of the Promontory apartment house, with its projecting wings, has been overshadowed by the abstract purity of the towers at 860 Lake Shore Drive. Perhaps that is why many of Mies' students were unprepared for the complicated massing of the Seagram office building. Occupying a block frontage on Park Avenue, the building stands on a pink granite podium and is set back one hundred feet from the sidewalk. It is a thirty-eight story tower sheathed in amber-gray glass and bronze. At the back of the tower a narrow projecting spine rises the full height: at the lower floors it is joined to small flanking wings. The grouping of these elements, including the podium, serves to make the tower itself emphatically frontal. This is one of the very few skyscrapers to have elevations identifiable as front, back, and sides; and yet this is accomplished without sacrificing the uniform clarity of its structural system or of the glass skin with which it is covered. The Seagram building elaborates structural themes stated at 860 Lake Shore Drive. Its dark bronze ages well: it is the first large building by Mies in America to match the standards of craftsmanship and fine materials characteristic of his European work.

The Seagram tower was Mies' first work in New York, and for this commission he chose to collaborate with Philip Johnson. In 1947, as director of the Department of Architecture at the Museum of Modern Art, Johnson had organized a major exhibition and written the first book devoted to Mies' work. Even before he left the Museum in 1954 to devote himself entirely to his architectural practice, Johnson was regarded as the most gifted advocate of Miesian ideas. The detailed conception of the Seagram project is entirely the work of Mies: its correspondingly fine interiors were a contribution of Johnson's.

Mies has preferred the linear (and decorative) possibilities of steel. Concrete was used in the Promontory apartment house as a substitute for steel, with no effort to develop characteristics peculiar to concrete alone. Many aspects of his use of structure are part of *de Stijl* aesthetics. Vertical elements attach to the thin edges of horizontal planes. The actual manner of fastening is concealed: pieces seem to adhere by magnetism. In a multi-story tower it is apparent that the mullions are semi-structural appliqués, if only because columns are larger and stand clear at the ground. But the same relationship of by-passing horizontal and vertical lines is employed in the small Farnsworth House of 1950. Heavy steel columns are welded, like the apartment house mullions, to the edges of three horizontal planes: a floor, a detached terrace, and the roof. Exquisite details and flawless craftsmanship serve to make this building one of the most dramatic statements of the Miesian idea. It has the intensity of the Barcelona Pavilion. Nothing detracts from its perfect expression of structure: there is nothing left to detract.

The metamorphosis of decorative mullion into structural column is completed in the Row House project of 1951. An example of this design, constructed as a private house, uses many steel columns welded to the edge of the roof and also to the steel edge of the floor slab; the columns do not touch the ground. The Row House might be a small section of the Lake Shore Drive towers lifted out of context and magnified in scale and elegance of finish.

Mies has carried the apparent simplification of structure to what must be its extreme limits in his 1951 project for a house "50 x 50 feet square." Because the roof is a grid of steel coffers welded to steel plates, it can be cantilevered from a single column in the exact center of each elevation. In this design, as in the Farnsworth house, interior divisions of space are created by low walls of closets and by a utility core housing bathrooms, kitchen and heating equipment. "Rooms" are the spaces between these elements. In the Farnsworth house the ceiling plane is a flat plaster surface masking steel beams: here it is added to the domain of pure structure. But the near disappearance of columns presents a fresh ambiguity: the building may be considered as being without corners, the flat face of each column constituting a "facade"; or as nothing but corners.

IN BUILDINGS designed for quite different purposes Mies has appeared to be concerned with structure alone. But a study of these buildings in chronological sequence suggests that the articulation of structure may be secondary to an even more compelling impulse: the reduction of all kinds of buildings to a single archetype. The 50 x 50 house is a *piano* sketch for what ought to be a gigantic and probably public space: a small residence, which must inevitably be sub-divided, however freely, does not require a clear span, and Mies' solution along these lines can be understood only in the sense that for him all architecture ought to conform to a single image. For Mies, as for many others, twentieth-century technology's most significant architectural image is the clear span at giant scale. With this as the central fact of architecture, it would seem that in Mies' view every other consideration must be refracted through the prism of technology.

One of Mies' most beautiful and problematic buildings illustrates perfectly the difficulty of phrasing a specific program so that it allows a clear-span structure. The 1952 Architecture and Design Building for Illinois Institute of Technology seems to be a single great room 120 x 210 feet. Exterior steel columns carry deep steel girders from which the roof is hung. The room is subdivided by a few low partitions. Two structures enclosing mechanical equipment and carrying ducts through the roof are set to the left and right of the entrance axis, but closer to the rear of the room: their placement is intended to make them clearly non-structural. Since the great room is used by many architecture classes, which with some self-discipline can manage not to impinge on one another's privacy, the arrangement is not altogether arbitrary. Its chief reward is the exhilaration of great scale.

But unfortunately this room accommodates only architecture students; design students are relegated to a basement floor with windows at grade level. The basement area is conventionally subdivided into access corridors and small classrooms.

Internal columns in a regular bay system carry the floor of the Architecture room above. From outside, however, the monumental scale of the steel girders automatically suggests that the floor, as well as the roof plane, is suspended, which is not the case. The inclusion of a lighted basement allows Mies to elevate the floor of the great room and thus to justify a handsome platform and steps leading to it.

Without actually being raised free of the ground, the building yet seems to be lifted up on itself. Its emphatic roof structure gives it that industrial character shared by all of Mies' buildings at Illinois Institute of Technology, from the boiler plant to the chapel, but here the prosaic is abruptly transformed into a singular poetic image.

In a 1953 project for a National Theatre at Mannheim, Germany, Mies brought together ideas explored in the Farnsworth house, the steel and glass apartment houses in Chicago, and the School of Architecture at Illinois Institute of Technology. The theatre is an enormous glass box held above ground. Unlike the Architecture School, the lower level is set back and clearly differentiated from the glass unit above: its marble walls extend to form an entrance court. As in the Architecture School, the roof is suspended, but this time from open trusses. Mies has here introduced diagonals to a structural aesthetic in which previously they played no part. Within the glass box two theatres are appended to one large unit housing a variety of services. This unit is a building itself, like the utility core of the Farnsworth house. But here it is the reality of the building, taking more space than the theatres. What remains on the perimeter serves as glass-enclosed promenade or portico.

The glass box is now simply a container unaffected by the activity within. Entrance to it is from below, an arrangement which preserves the uniformity of its elevations and also affords a suitable preparation for its great scale. The diagonals of the truss construction now relate it clearly to the pragmatic architecture of bridges and factories. Juxtaposed with marble and glass, the truss brings to the realm of fine architecture an astonishing vitality. Mies has developed each element in this design to its logical end, but part of the Mannheim project's significance is its ambiguity. The component parts are not determined by the specific function "theatre," but rather they are combined to form a vast enclosure which could well house other activities. Similarly, the Seagram office building and the Lake Shore Drive apartment houses are interchangeable. Like them, the Mannheim theatre goes beyond functionalism by avoiding the limitations of any particular function or program; instead it offers what has been called a "universal space."

ALL THESE THEMES are fused into a work of enormous power in the 1953 study for a Convention Hall, commissioned by Chicago's South Side Planning Board. In this project Mies brings architecture into the realm of heroic enterprise: the flat roof of the Convention Hall would span seven hundred and twenty feet (roughly two city blocks) without interior columns, at a height of one hundred and twelve feet. It is a steel truss built up on a module thirty feet in each direction and thirty feet deep. The square compartments thus formed are laterally braced on each plane. At the edge of the truss the bracing is carried down into the wall, which becomes itself a flat truss. The entire structure rests on tapered concrete columns one hundred and twenty feet apart, six to each elevation. The steel grid of its "walls" would be filled with marble or, in the final version, metal panels in two colors. The resulting diaper pattern has a vitality beyond the reach of purely rectilinear structures. Set in a vast open space and scaled to accommodate fifty thousand people, this building is a public artifact like a bridge or a dam.

With the Convention Hall project Mies accomplishes as never before the reduction of architecture to pure structure. Contributing to this is the nature of the project itself: complicated interior partitions are unnecessary, but the building is so large that its structure would in any case dominate whatever it contained. That the Convention Hall does not offer solutions to problems other than those of clear-span structure is suggested by the 1958 design for the Bacardi administration building in Havana, Cuba. Here again Mies proposes a coffered roof carried by perimeter columns, translating the Convention Hall into concrete. But for this smaller building a variety of spaces and services are required: to preserve the character of the great room Mies has deposited most of them in a basement. Such partitioning as is indispensable to the main room seems mechanically artful in its arrangement. Like the partially walled podium on which the building stands, it lacks the objective finality of the structure itself. The dialogue between space and structure, proceeding here by contrast, does not yield the intense image achieved in the Convention Hall. In that project structure is given its most direct and daring interpretation. Unbuilt, it remains the most monumental image twentieth-century architecture has yet produced.

TECHNOLOGY SEEMS to make possible anything we may think of. Most of these possibilities Mies has rejected. He has described his architecture as "skin and bones," and he has described his attitude toward art with the phrase "less is more." It is true that Mies has made architecture of steel bones and glass skin.

Fixing with a hard stare on a single thing, he has eliminated so much that seems irrelevant that what is left stands forth with unexpected significance.

More important perhaps than the things Mies retains is the process by which he selects them. The characteristic architectural space he devised in the 1920s could be developed most intensively along the horizontal plane. The Barcelona Pavilion, the Berlin building exposition house, and the court house projects channel space freely between free walls, but rigidly between fixed floor and roof planes. As a result Mies eliminated from this aesthetic all buildings with more than one floor. When his interest turned to the design of the structural skeleton, as in the first group of buildings for Illinois Institute of Technology, Mies brought multi-story buildings within the range of a single aesthetic. But except for the unbuilt Library and Administration Hall the structural system articulated only itself, excluding the possibility of developed space. Neither has Mies been concerned, since his first projects for glass skyscrapers, with an architectural aesthetic determined by the skin rather than the bones.

Mies' most original buildings are one-story structures, and the greatest of these consist of one room. In this sense Mies has designed nothing but temples, which is to say that he has revealed the irrational mainspring of our technological culture. The most recent of his buildings, unlike the late works of Frank Lloyd Wright, gain in relevance with each fresh assertion of originality. And unlike the late works of Le Corbusier, they confirm rather than repudiate their designer's initial dedication to an architecture of rational, communicable order.

In his seventy-third year Ludwig Mies van der Rohe commands the attention of architects throughout the world. Other points of view contest his own: since the end of World War II architects have been increasingly dissatisfied with the tight range of forms made possible by skeleton construction. They have sought especially to renew and amplify values of plastic form, through curvilinear shell construction in concrete or through the expressive elaboration of individual structural elements. Mies himself has not remained indifferent to such movements. The tapered concrete columns of the Convention Hall and the Bacardi administration building, for example, are structural forms of plastic, rather than linear, value.

The measure of Mies' authority is this: it no longer seems possible to rebel against the Miesian discipline except in Miesian terms: the alternatives to his philosophy are themselves based on the design of structure. With Mies architecture leaves childhood behind.

32

1. Office Building for Friedrichstasse, Berlin, 1919. Project (opposite page).

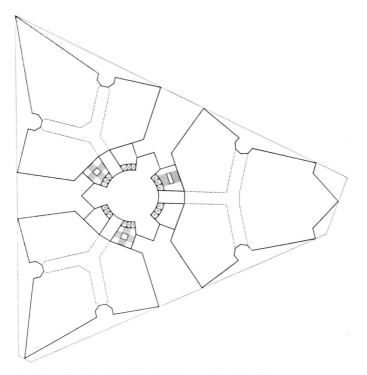

2. Office Building for Friedrichstrasse. Project. Plan.

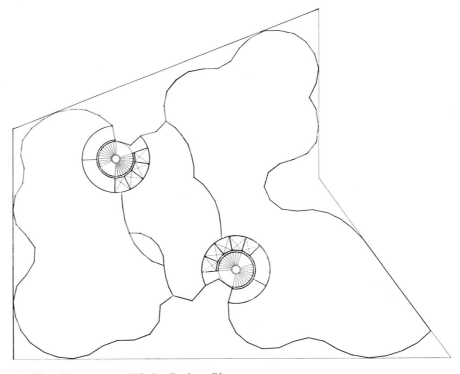

3. Glass Skyscraper, 1920–21. Project. Plan.

4. Glass Skyscraper. Project. Montage with model (opposite page).

5. Concrete Office Building, 1922. Project.

6, 7. Brick Country House, 1923. Project. Elevation (top) and plan (bottom).

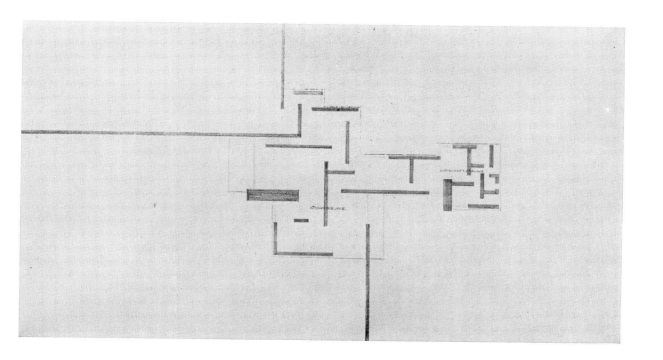

8. Concrete Country House, 1923. Project. General view.

9. Concrete Country House. Project.

10. Karl Liebknecht and Rosa Luxemburg Monument, Berlin, 1926. Demolished.

11. Wolf House, Guben, Germany, 1926. Terrace.

12. Wolf House.

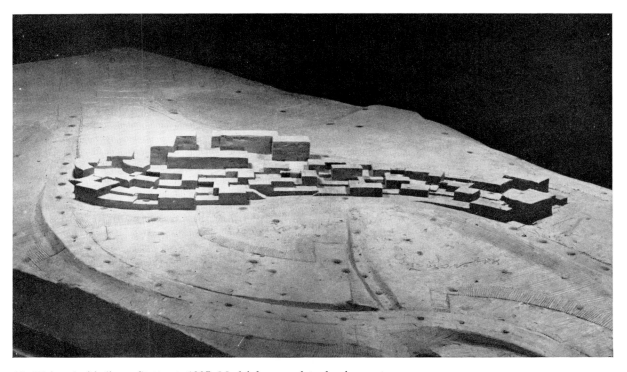

13. Weissenhofsiedlung, Stuttgart, 1927. Model for complete development.

14. Apartment House, Weissenhofsiedlung, Stuttgart, 1927.

16. Hermann Lange House, Krefeld, Germany, 1928.

15. Esters House, Krefeld, Germany, 1928 (opposite page).

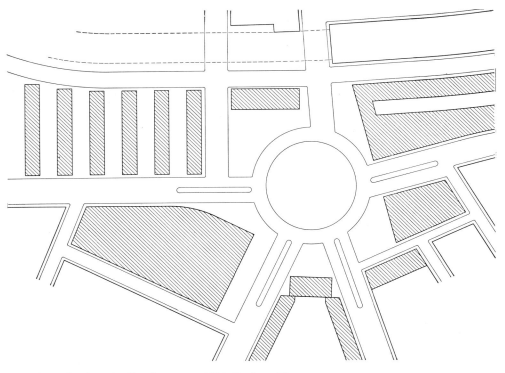

17. Alexanderplatz, Berlin, Germany, 1928. Project. Plan.

18. Alexanderplatz. Project.

19. Alexanderplatz. Project.

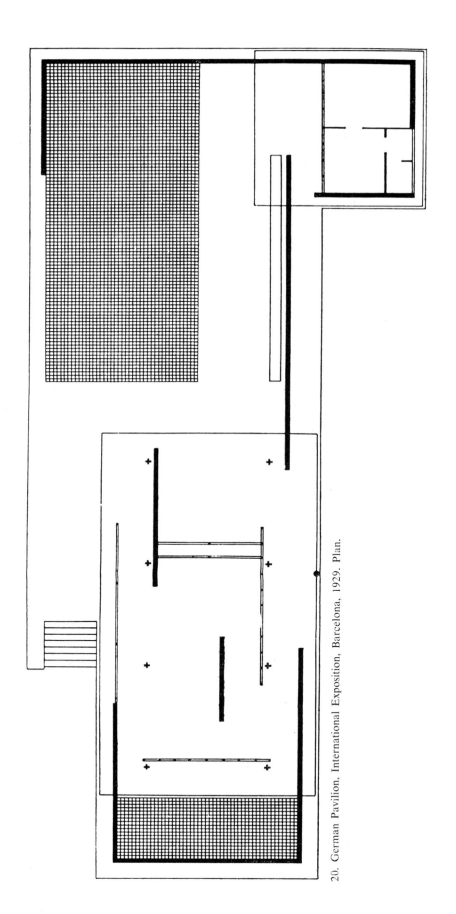

20. German Pavilion, International Exposition, Barcelona, 1929. Plan.

21. Barcelona Pavilion (opposite page).

22. Barcelona Pavilion.

23. Barcelona Pavilion.

24. Barcelona Pavilion.

25. Barcelona Pavilion (opposite page).

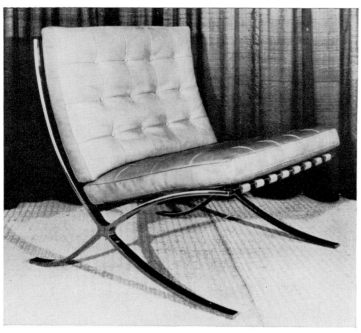

26. Barcelona chair. 1929.

28. "Brno" chair, 1930.

29. "Tugendhat" chair, 1930.

30. "Conchoidal" chair. 1946. For production in plastic.

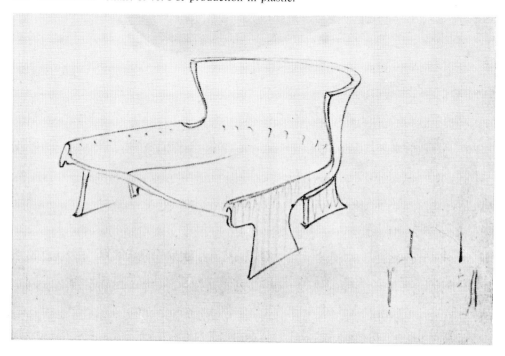

31. Silk Exhibit of the Exposition de la Mode, Berlin, 1927 (opposite page).

32. Glass Industry Exhibit of the Werkbund Exposition, Stuttgart, 1927.

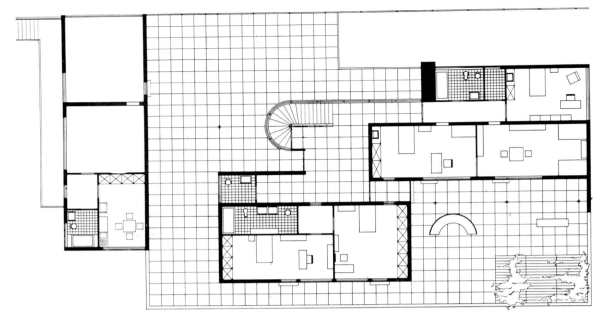

33. Tugendhat House. Upper story plan.

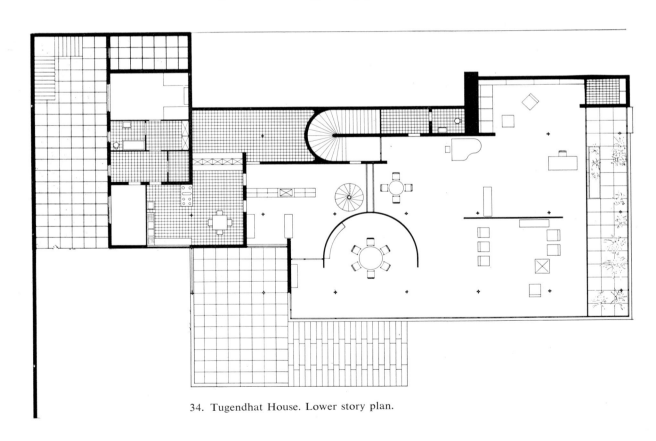

34. Tugendhat House. Lower story plan.

35. Tugendhat House, Brno, Czechoslovakia, 1930.

36. Tugendhat House.

37. Tugendhat House.

38. Tugendhat House (opposite page).

39. Tugendhat House.

40. Tugendhat House.

41. Tugendhat House.

42. Tugendhat House.

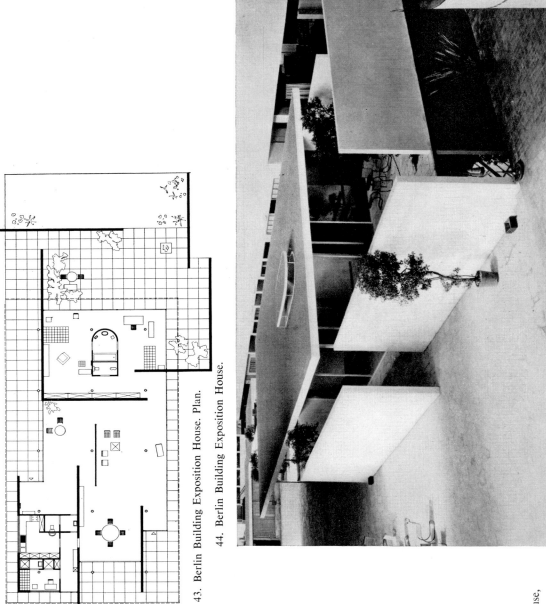

43. Berlin Building Exposition House. Plan.

44. Berlin Building Exposition House.

45. Berlin Building Exposition House, 1931 (opposite page).

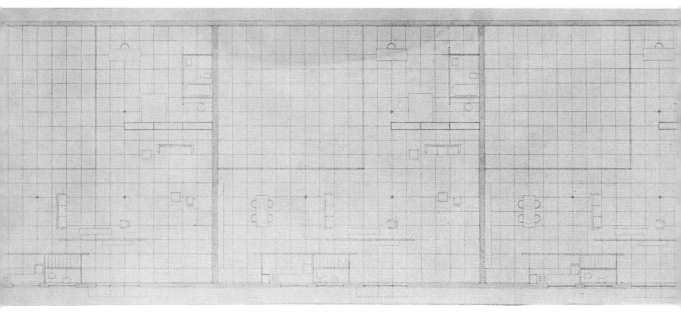

46. Row House, 1931. Project. Plan.

47. Row House. Project. Montage drawing of interior.

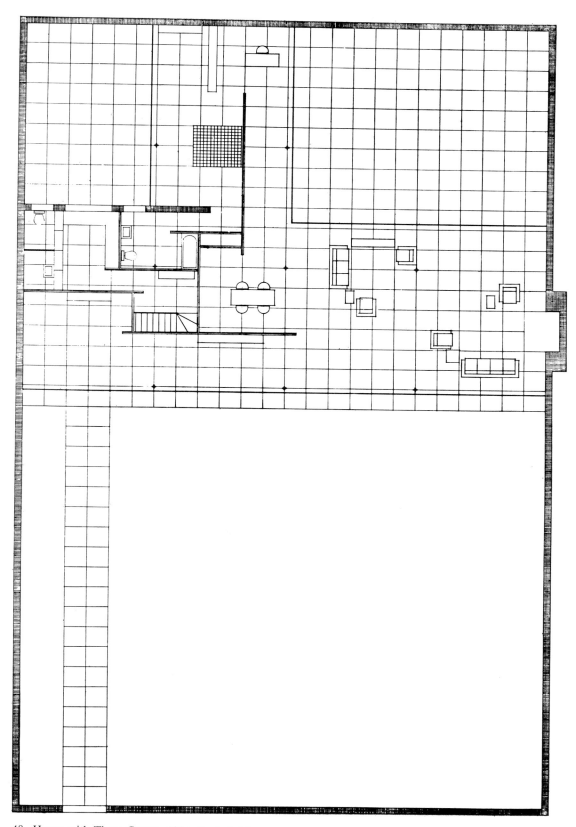

48. House with Three Courts, 1934. Project. Plan.

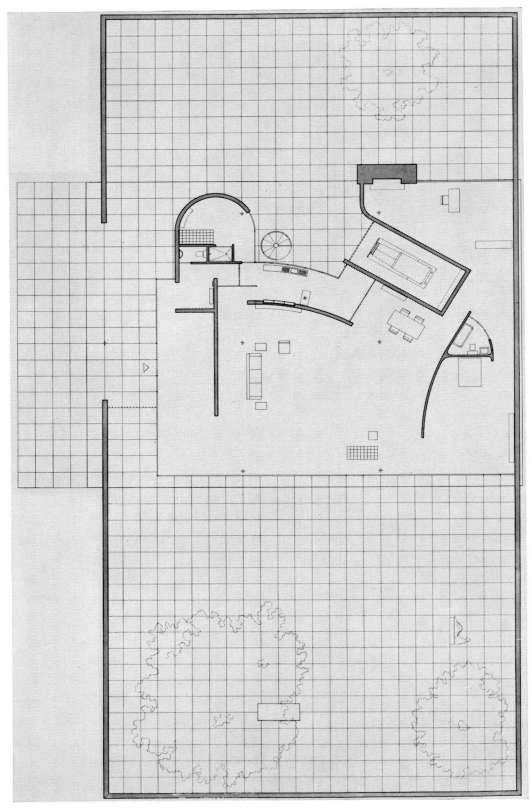

49. Court House with garage, 1934. Project. Plan.

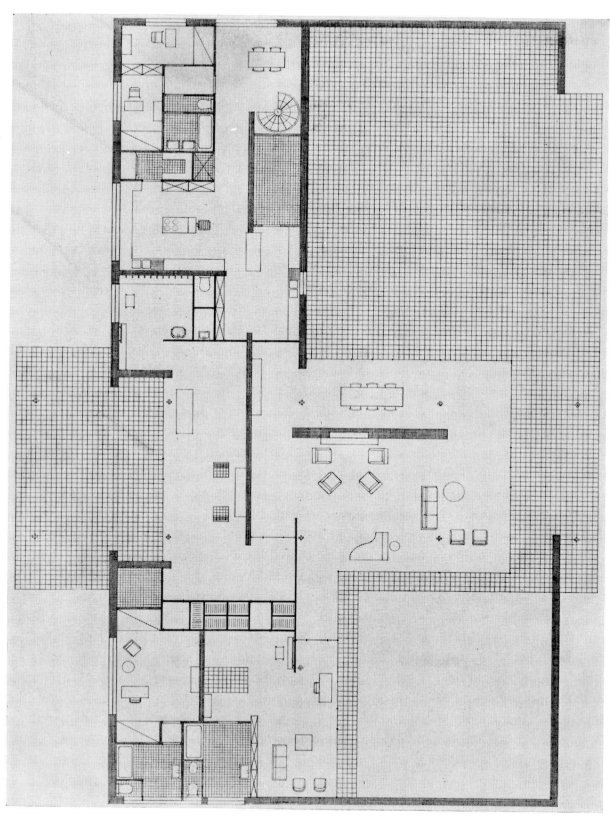

50. Hubbe House, Magdeburg, Germany, 1935. Project. Plan.

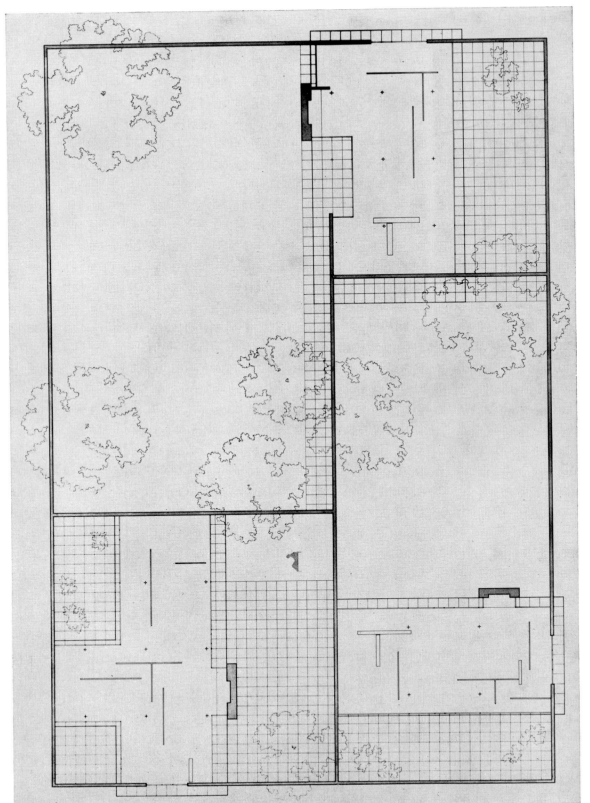

51. Group of Three Court Houses, 1938. Project. Plan.

52. Group of Three Court Houses. Project. Model.

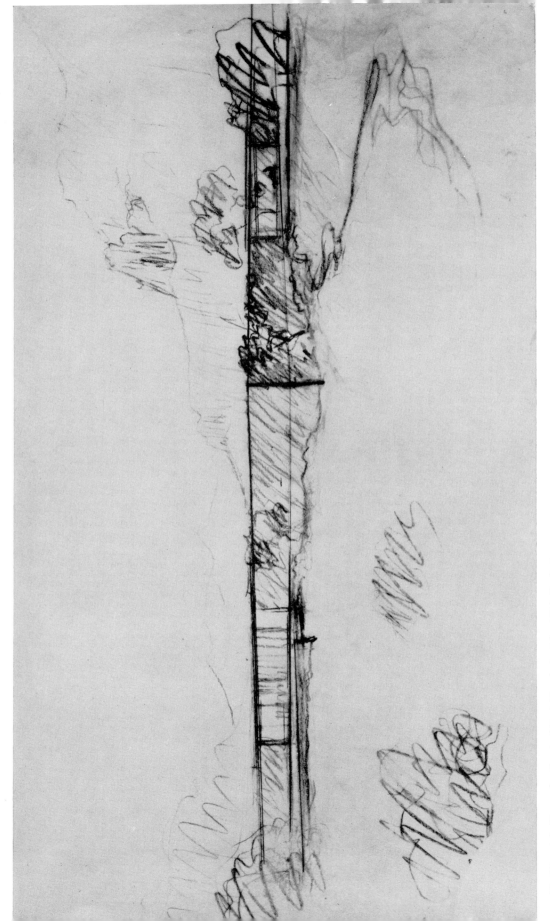

53. Mountain House for the Architect, Tyrol, Austria, 1934. Project.

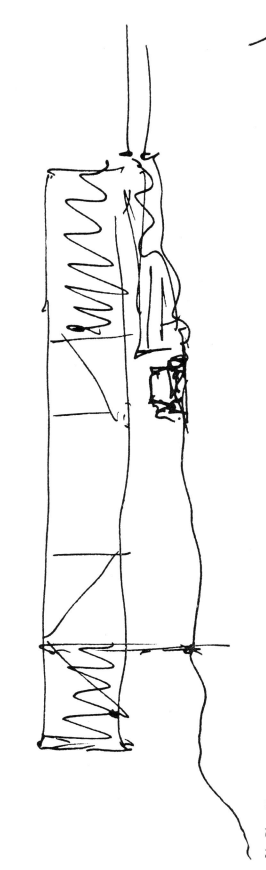

54. Glass House on a Hillside, ca. 1934. Project. Elevation.

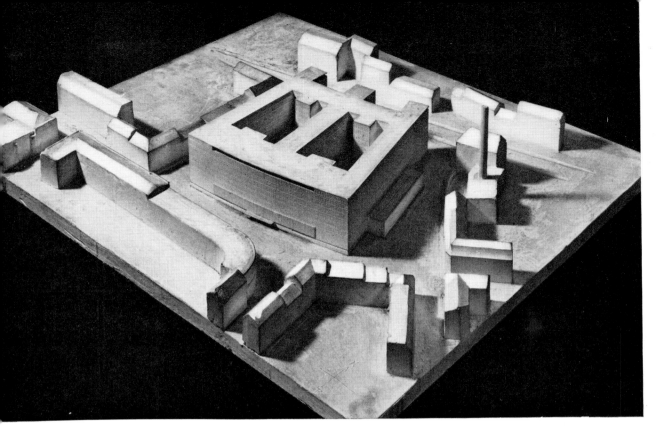

55. Reichsbank, Berlin, 1933. Project. Model.

56. Administration Building for the Silk Industry, Krefeld, Germany, 1937. Project. Model.

57. Resor House, Jackson Hole, Wyoming, 1938. Project.

58. House on Two Levels, 1938. Project.

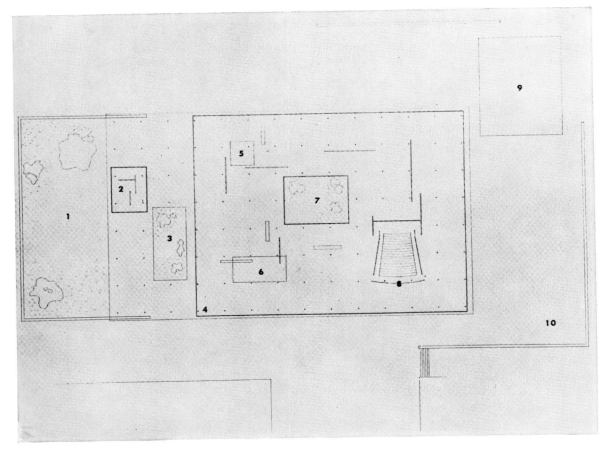

59. Museum for a Small City, 1942. Project. Plan.

60. Museum for a Small City. Project. Montage drawing of interior.

61. Concert Hall, 1942. Project.

62. Illinois Institute of Technology, Chicago, Illinois. Model.

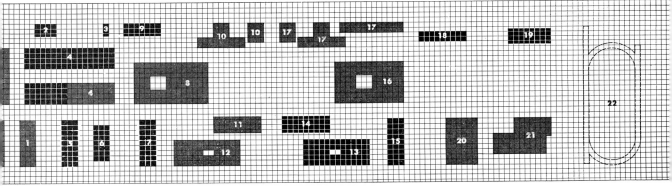

63. Illinois Institute of Technology, 1940. Final plan.

Gray indicates future buildings; black indicates completed buildings.

1. Armour Research Foundation Research Laboratory
2. Boiler Plant
3. Central Vault
4. A.R.F. Engineering Research
5. Institute of Gas Technology Laboratory
6. Institute of Gas Technology
7. School of Architecture and Design
8. Student Union and Auditorium
9. Minerals and Metals Research
10. Electrical Engineering and Physics
11. Lewis Institute
12. Mechanical Engineering
13. Chemical Engineering and Metallurgy
14. Chemistry
15. Alumni Memorial Hall
16. Library and Administration
17. Civil Engineering and Mechanics
18. Association of American Railroads Building
19. Association of American Railroads Laboratory
20. Field House
21. Gymnasium and Swimming Pool
22. Athletic Field

64. Illinois Institute of Technology. (Left) Alumni Memorial Hall, (center) Chemical and Metallurgy Building, (right) Chemistry Building, 1940.

65. Illinois Institute of Technology, Minerals and Metals Research Building, 1942–43.

66. Minerals and Metals Research Building.

67. Illinois Institute of Technology, Alumni Memorial Hall, 1945–46.

68. Alumni Memorial Hall. Corner detail.

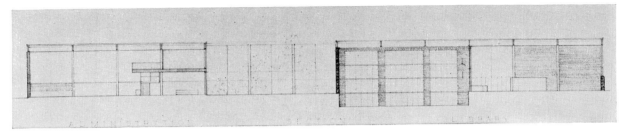

69. Illinois Institute of Technology, Library and Administration Building, 1944. Project. Longitudinal section.

70. Library and Administration Building. Project. Model.

71. Library and Administration Building. Project.

73. Illinois Institute of Technology, Chapel, 1952.

72. Illinois Institute of Technology, Boiler Plant, 1950 (opposite page).

74. Chapel. Interior.

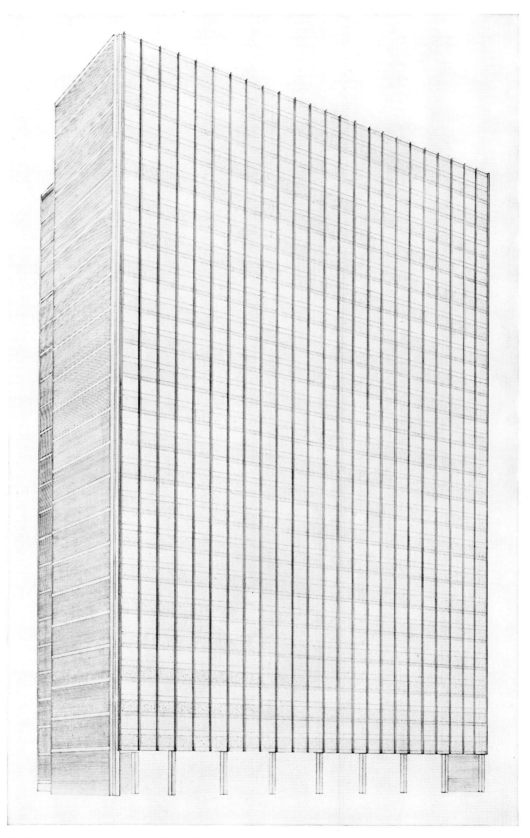

75. Promontory Apartments. Project in steel.

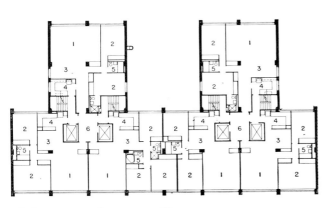

76. Promontory Apartments. Plan.

77. Promontory Apartments, 1949. Concrete.

78. Farnsworth House, Plano, Illinois, 1950.

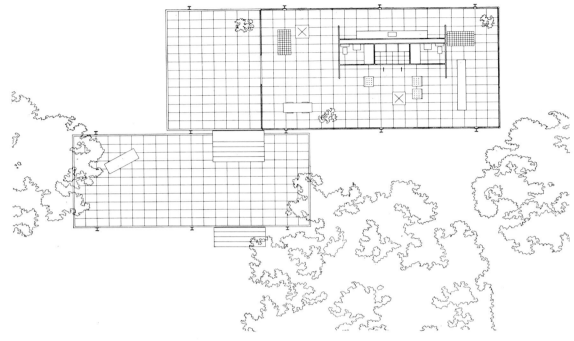

79. Farnsworth House. Plan.

80. Farnsworth House.

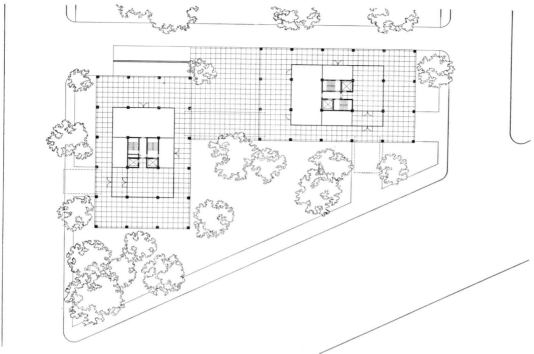

81. Apartment House, 860 Lake Shore Drive. Plan.

82. Apartment House, 860 Lake Shore Drive, Chicago, Illinois, 1951.

83. Apartment House, 860 Lake Shore Drive (opposite page).

85. Commonwealth Promenade, Chicago, Illinois, 1957. Model.

86. Gratiot Avenue Housing Development, Detroit, Michigan, 1957–. Model.

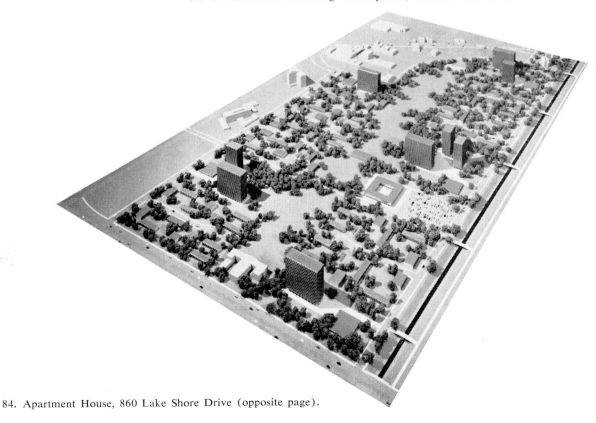

84. Apartment House, 860 Lake Shore Drive (opposite page).

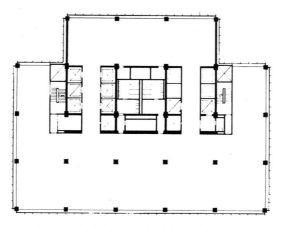

87. Seagram Building. Typical floor plan.

88. Seagram Building. Ground floor plan.

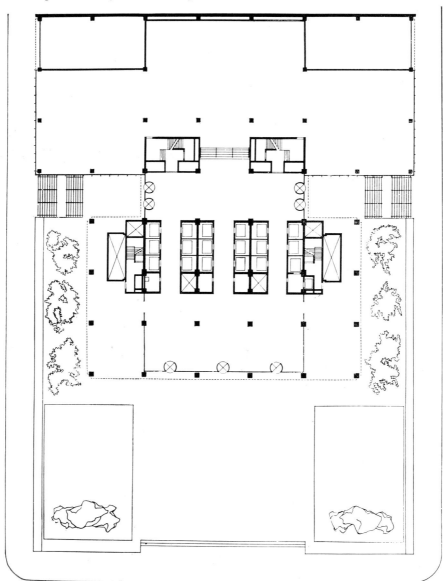

89. Seagram Building, 375 Park Avenue, New York, 1958.

90. Seagram Building.

91. Seagram Building.

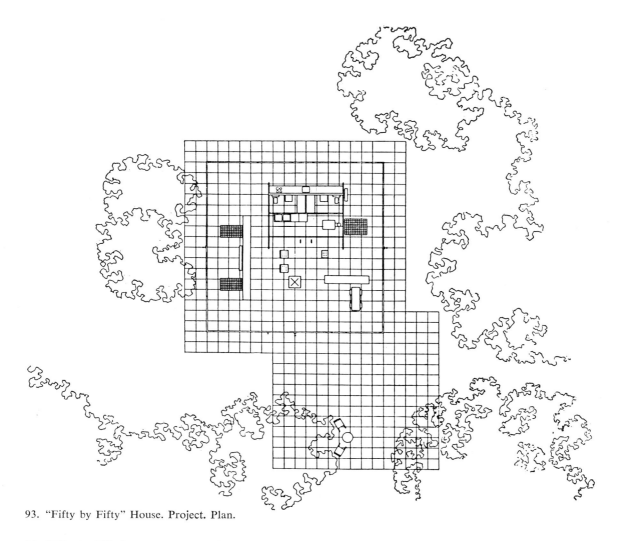

93. "Fifty by Fifty" House. Project. Plan.

94. "Fifty by Fifty" House, 1951. Project. Model.

92. Row House Prototype, Chicago, 1951 (opposite page).

95. Drive-in restaurant, 1949. Project. Model.

96. Illinois Institute of Technology, School of Architecture and Design, 1952 (opposite page).

97. School of Architecture and Design.

98. School of Architecture and Design (opposite page).

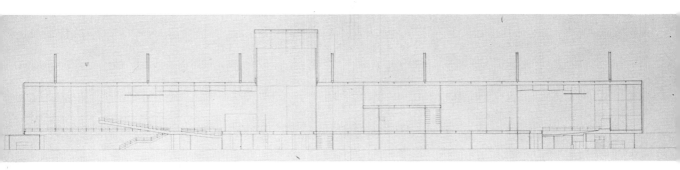

99. National Theatre. Project. Longitudinal section.

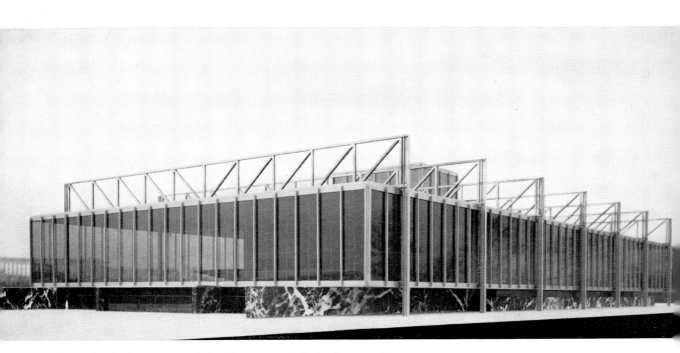

100. National Theatre, Mannheim, Germany, 1953. Project. Model.

101. National Theatre. Project. Model.

102. Convention Hall, Chicago, 1953. Project. Montage-drawing.

103. Convention Hall. Project. Model.

104. Convention Hall. Project. Detail of Model.

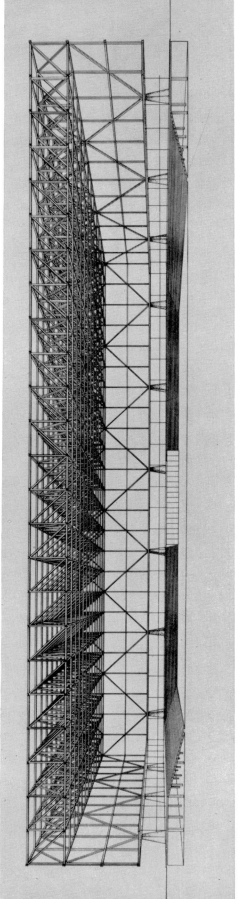

105. Convention Hall. Project. Cross-section and perspective.

106. Convention Hall. Montage of interior (opposite page).

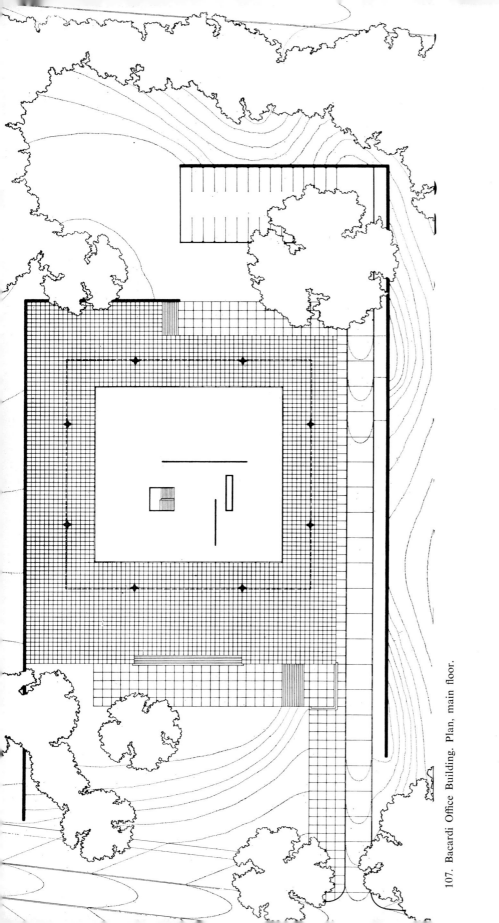

107. Bacardi Office Building. Plan, main floor.

108. Bacardi Office Building. Longitudinal section.

109. Bacardi Office Building, Santiago de Cuba. Under construction. Model.

110. Bacardi Office Building. Montage-drawing, interior.

111. Bacardi Office Building. Model.

CHRONOLOGY

1886   Born in Aachen, Germany
1897   Completed attendance at Cathedral School, Aachen
1802–1804   Designer-draftsman with local architects
1905–1907   Apprenticed to cabinet maker Bruno Paul in Berlin
1907   Left Bruno Paul to execute his first commission
1908–1911   Draftsman in the office of Peter Behrens
1912   Spent a year in The Hague to work on design for Kröller House
1912–1914   Returned to independent architectural practice in Berlin
1914–1918   Military service
1919–1938   Own architectural practice in Berlin
1926–1932   Held office as first vice-president of Deutscher Werkbund
1927   Directed the Werkbund Exposition in Stuttgart
1929   Built the German Pavilion at the International Exposition in Barcelona
1930   Appointed director of the Bauhaus in Dessau
1933   Closed the Bauhaus because of political pressure
1938   Emigrated to the United States, appointed Director of Architecture at Armour Institute (later the Illinois Institute of Technology) in Chicago
1958   Retired from the Illinois Institute of Technology to take up full time private practice in Chicago
1959   Awarded gold medal, Royal Institute of British Architects

SELECTED CHRONOLOGICAL LIST OF
BUILDINGS AND PROJECTS (1907–1959)

1907   Riehl House, Berlin
1911   Perls House, Berlin
1912   Kröller House, The Hague, Holland (Project)
1919   Office Building for Friedrichstrasse, Berlin (Project)
1921   Glass Skyscraper (Project)
1922   Concrete Office Building, Berlin (Project)
1923   Brick Country House (Project)
1924   Concrete Country House (Project)
1926   Karl Liebknecht and Rosa Luxemburg Monument, Berlin (Demolished)
       Wolf House, Guben, Germany
1927   Apartment House, Weissenhofsiedlung, Stuttgart, Germany
       Silk Exhibit for Exposition de la Mode, Berlin
       Glass Industry Exhibit, Werkbund Exposition, Stuttgart, Germany
1928   Alexanderplatz remodeling, Berlin (Project)
       Esters House, Krefeld, Germany
       Hermann Lange House, Krefeld, Germany
1929   German Pavilion, International Exposition, Barcelona
1930   Tugendhat House, Brno, Czechoslovakia
1931   House, Berlin Building Exposition, Berlin
       Row House (Project)
1933   Reichsbank, Berlin (Project)
1934   House with three courts (Project)
       Court house with garage (Project)
       Mountain house for the architect, Tyrol, Austria (Project)
       Glass house on a hillside (Project)
1935   Hubbe House, Magdeburg, Germany (Project)
1937   Administration building for the Silk Industry, Krefeld, Germany (Project)

1938   Group of three court houses (Project)
       Resor House, Jackson Hole, Wyoming (Project)
       House on two levels (Project)
1939–1940   Plans for the new campus at the Illinois Institute of Technology,
       Chicago, Illinois. Buildings already completed include:
       1942–1943   Minerals and Metals Research Building
       1945–1946   Alumni Memorial Hall
       1946   Metallurgy and Chemical Engineering Building
       1950   Boiler Plant
       1952   Chapel
       1956   School of Architecture and Design
1942   Museum for a small city (Project)
       Concert Hall (Project)
1946   Drive-in Restaurant (Project)
1949   Promontory Apartments, Chicago, Illinois
1950   Farnsworth House, Plano, Illinois
1951   Apartment Houses, 860 Lake Shore Drive, Chicago, IIIinois
       Row House, Chicago, Illinois
       Fifty by Fifty House (Project)
1953   National Theatre, Mannheim, Germany (Project)
       Convention Hall, Chicago (Project)
       Commonwealth Promenade Apartment Houses, Chicago, Illinois
1957   Lafayette Park Housing Development, Detroit, Michigan
1958   Seagram Building, 375 Park Avenue, New York City
1958   Bacardi Office Building, Santiago de Cuba (under construction in 1959)

BIBLIOGRAPHY OF ARTICLES
WRITTEN BY MIES VAN DER ROHE

"Hochhausprojekt für Bahnhof Friedrich-Strasse in Berlin," *Frühlicht* No. 1, 1922.

"Bürohaus," *G* (Berlin), June, 1923.

"Baukunst und zeitwille." *Der Querschnitt* No. 4, 1924.

"Industrielles Bauen," *G* (Berlin), No. 3, 1924.

"Briefe an die form," *Die Form* No. 1, 1926.

"Zum neuen jahrgang [an Dr. Riezler]," *Die Form* No. 1, 1927.

"Rundschau: zum neuen jahrgang [an Dr. Riezler]," *Die Form* No. 2, 1927.

"Introduction to issue devoted to 'Werkbundausstellung die wohnung Stuttgart 1927'," *Die Form* No. 9, 1927.

"Vorwort, Zu Meinem Block; Bau und Wohnung: die Bauten der Weissenhofsiedlung in Stuttgart errichtet," *Deutscher Werkbund,* Stuttgart, 1927.

"Zum Thema: Ausstellungen," *Die Form* No. 4, 1928.

"Über kunstkritik," *Das Kunstblatt,* June, 1930.

"Die neue zeit: Schlussworte des referats Mies van der Rohe auf der wiener tagung des deutschen werkbundes," *Die Form* No. 1, 1930.

"Introduction," in Ludwig Hilberseimer, *The New City*. Theobald, Chicago, 1944.

"A tribute to Frank Lloyd Wright," *College Art Journal,* Autumn 1946.

SELECTED BIBLIOGRAPHY ON
MIES VAN DER ROHE

"Bacardi Building, Cuba. Mies's one-office office building," *Architectural Forum,* February, 1959.

Behrendt, Walter Curt, "Mies van der Rohe," *Magazine of Art,* October 1939.

———— *Modern Building, its Nature, Problems, and Forms.* Harcourt, Brace, New York, 1937.

———— "Skyscrapers in Germany," *Journal of the American Institute of Architects,* September 1923.

Bier, Justus, "Mies van der Rohes Reichspavillon in Barcelona," *Die Form* August 15, 1929.

Blake, Peter, "Modern architecture; the difficult art of simplicity," *Architectural Forum,* May 1958.

"Chicago Apartments. Eight projects; Commonwealth Promenade and 900 Esplanade; I.I.T. housing," *Architectural Forum,* November 1955.

"Chicago Convention Hall," *Architectural Forum,* December 1953.

Creighton, Thomas H., "Seagram house re-assessed," *Progressive Architecture,* June 1959.

"Crown Hall, I.I.T.," *Architectural Forum,* August 1956.

"Cullinan Wing, Houston Museum," *Arts and Architecture,* July 1959.

Dearstyne, Howard, "Basic teaching of architecture," *Liturgical Arts,* May 1944.

Doesburg, Theo van, "Die neue Architektur und ihre Folgen," *Wasmuths Monatshefte für Baukunst,* September 1925.

Drexler, Arthur, "Seagram building." *Architectural Record,* July 1958.

"Ein Werk des Neuen Bauens unter Denkmalschutz," *Werk,* September 1955.

Eisler, Max, "Mies van der Rohe: eine Villa in Brünn," *Bau und Werkkunst,* August 1932.

"Emergence of a master architect," *Life,* March 18, 1957.

"Exposition Internationale du Bâtiment à Berlin, 1931; La Maison Tugendhat à Brünn, 1931," *Architecture Vivante,* Winter 1931.

"Farnsworth House," *Architectural Forum,* October 1951.

"Genetrix; Personal contributions to American architecture," *Architectural Review,* May 1957.

Genzmer, Walther, "Der deutsche Reichspavillon auf der Internationalen Ausstellung, Barcelona," *Die Baugilde,* November 1929.

Gravenkamp, Curt, "Mies van der Rohe: Glashaus in Berlin," *Das Kunstblatt,* April 1930.

Grohmann, Will, "Mies van der Rohe," *Allgemeines Lexikon der beldenden Künstler,* 1930.

Hegemann, Werner, "Künstlerische Tagesfragen bei Bau von Einfamilienhäusern . . . Flaches und schräges Dach," *Wasmuths Monatshefts für Baukunst,* March 1927.

Hilberseimer, Ludwig, *Mies van der Rohe,* P. Theobald, Chicago, 1956.

Hitchcock, Henry-Russell, "Berlin Architectural Show, 1931," *Hound & Horn,* October–December, 1931.

——— *Modern Architecture, Romanticism and Reintegration.* Payson & Clarke, New York, 1929.

——— "The evolution of Wright, Mies and Le Corbusier," *Perspecta,* Summer, 1952.

——— and Johnson, Philip, *The International Style: Architecture since 1922.* W. W. Norton, New York, 1932.

"I.I.T. Building for the college of architecture, planning and design, Illinois Institute of Technology," *Arts and Architecture,* August 1954; see also *Architectural Record,* July 1954 and January 1955; *Progressive Architecture,* July 1955.

Johnson, Philip C., *Mies van der Rohe.* Museum of Modern Art New York, 1953.

——— "The Berlin Building Exposition of 1931," *Shelter,* January, 1932.

Jordy, William H., "Seagram assessed, with a footnote by P. Smithson," *Architectural Review,* December 1958.

Korn, Arthur, *Glas in Bau und als Gebrauchsgegenstand,* Berlin-Charlottenburg, E. Pollak [1928]?

"L'oeuvre de Mies van der Rohe," *Art et Décoration* No. 40, 1954.

Lopez, R., "Visite aux U.S.A., la leçon de Mies van der Rohe," *Architecture d'Aujourd'hui,* February 1959.

"Mannheim Theatre; proposed national theatre for the city of Mannheim," *Arts and Architecture,* July 1954. See also H. Curjel, "Die Mannheimer theaterprojekte." *Werk,* October 1953; *Architecture d'Aujourd'hui,* January 1954; *Architectural Forum,* July 1953.

"Metals and Minerals Research Building, Illinois Institute of Technology," *Architectural Forum,* November 1943.

"Mies van der Rohe, architecte," *Architecture d'Aujourd'hui,* June 1947.

"Mies van der Rohe, Conversations regarding the future of architecture," Excerpt from the 1. p. record, *Print,* February 1957.

Mies van der Rohe, Ludwig, "Architecture and Technology." [Three addresses at the Blackstone Hotel, April 17, 1950 on the occasion of the celebration of the addition of the Institute of Design to Illinois Institute of Technology.) *Interiors,* December, 1952.

Mumford, Lewis. "Skyline: the lesson of the master." *New Yorker,* September 13, 1958.

"Museum. Mies van der Rohe, architect." *Architectural Forum,* May 1943. Project: Explanatory text by Mies van der Rohe.

Nelson, George. "Architects of Today" . . . *Pencil Points,* September, 1935.

Cubism and abstract art. Museum of Modern Art, New York, 1932.

"Le Problème des Formes des Places Mondiales, Alexanderplatz, 1928; exposition de Stuttgart, 1927," *Architecture Vivante,* Autumn 1929.

Roth, Alfred, "Bermerkungen zu den Wohnhoch-häusern von Mies van der Rohe in Chicago," *Werk,* January 1951.

"Thirteen Housing Developments," *Architectural Forum,* March 1932.

Wachsmann, Konrad, "Mies van der Rohe, his work," *Arts and Architecture,* March 1952.

Westheim, Paul, in *Helden und Abenteurer.* "Mies van der Rohe, charaktervoll Bauen." Berlin, Reckendorf, 1931.

Wright, E., "Van der Rohe's steel," *Architectural Forum,* September 1953.

Zevi, Bruno, "Mies van der Rohe e Frank Ll. Wright, poeti dello spazio," *Metron,* July–August 1950.

SOURCES OF ILLUSTRATIONS

Bill Engdahl, Hedrich-Blessing, Chicago, Illinois: 84, 86, 103
Alexander Georges, New City, New York: 91
Bill Hedrich, Hedrich-Blessing, Chicago, Illinois: 100, 101
Hedrich-Blessing, Chicago, Illinois: 2, 3, fig. 5, 17, 19, 31, 33, 34, 43, 46, 49, 50, 53, 55, 56, 64–68, 72–75, 77–83, 87, 88, 92, 94, 95, 97, 104, 107, 108, 110
Courtesy Museum of Modern Art, New York: figs. 1, 2, 6, 7, 8, (George Barrows), 9; 1, 4, 6–16, 18, 21, 22, 24, 25, 30, 32, 35–39, 40, 41, 45, 51, 52 (Herbert Matter), 54, 57 (Soichi Sunami), 61, 63, 70, 76, 93, 98, 99, 102, 106
George H. Steuer, Oconomowoc, Wisconsin: 85
Ezra Stoller, Rye, New York: 89, 90
Suter, Hedrich-Blessing, Chicago, Illinois: 109, 111
United States Steel Corporation, New York: fig. 10
Williams and Meyer, Chicago, Illinois: 5, 20, 23, 42, 47, 48, 59, 60, 69, 71

INDEX

The numerals in *italics* refer to the illustrations.